The Phoenix Living Poets

———◦◦◦◦◦◦◦———

DAYLIGHT ASTRONOMY

The Phoenix Living Poets

★

DAYLIGHT ASTRONOMY

by

Edward Lowbury

CHATTO AND WINDUS

THE HOGARTH PRESS

1968

Published by
Chatto and Windus Ltd
with The Hogarth Press Ltd
42 William IV Street
London WC2
*
Clarke, Irwin and Co Ltd
Toronto

Acknowledgments are made to the Editors of
Encounter, *Alta*, *The Western Mail*, *Extra Verse*, to the
B.B.C. Third Programme and Home Service
(Midland); also to Roy Lewis of the *Keepsake Press*
for five poems from *New Poems*.

SBN 7011 1325 1

© Edward Lowbury 1968

Printed in Great Britain by
William Lewis (Printers) Limited
Cardiff

FOR ALISON

Contents

THE COLLECTOR

Let loose at five in a wood loud with bluebells
I thought "How fine if I could grab the lot",
And set about picking them — did nothing else
For half the morning; but the sun was hot
And the greenwood still alive with bluebells;
By the time they called me home
I saw how much I would have to do without.

So the next time they put me out to grass
The plan was simpler: I would pick one flower
Of every kind. Soon my hands were full;
I looked around, and there were plenty more —
Far more than I could carry in my head;
But glancing down at those which I had gathered,
I noticed some were dead.

So again there was something I must do without!
It seemed I should confine myself to the names
And leave the plants when next a frenzy
Goaded me to collect; but of all games
This was the craziest: there were always more
Than I could gather, and others beyond reach;
And the more I had, the less I knew of each.

A lifetime brought this new collector's itch:
In a world of flowers, names, necessities —
To see how many I could do without:
And at last the distant shout
"Come home" finds me exulting in a wealth
Of unpossessions — all of it, perhaps,
A practice-run for doing without myself.

SNAPSHOT

When something holds my breath —
Rare peak, rose, angel,
Shots of eternity —
I reach for my camera;
Too busy now to savour
The revelation, I store it;
A permanent record seems right
For the eternal moment.

But these transparencies
Have missed the only tricks
That took my breath — transience,
Presence, perpetual change.
Their lightning is congealed,
Not stored; their permanence
Not ghost, but skeleton.
My aim was all right —
Rose, angel, peak are there,
But the smooth bored camera
Has shot them stone dead —
Almost as if, in anger,
I had reached for my gun.

THE THUNDER BIRD

This wooded hill was once a sacred mountain:
"Little Saanich Mountain", the Indians called it,
And the name survives. On top, the thunder bird
Built his nest. No-one ever saw him,
But everyone knew the flashing of his eyes
And the thunder of his wings which shook the earth
When clouds hid the peak on sultry days.
Children trembled to hear how from his eyrie
The thunder bird ranged and plucked whales
Out of the sea and carried them in his talons
Back to the mountain, where he feasted on them.

Now on the same hill, that silver dome –
At a glance you might mistake it for a mosque –
Is an astrophysical observatory; its eye,
A seventy-inch reflector, at one time
The sharpest on this planet, penetrates
Into the farthest reaches of the Universe
And brings back messages well worth recording –
The size and composition of galaxies
And the probable origin of all existence.
At week-ends the curious may come in
To be shown the rings of Saturn, the Milky Way,
The distant nebulae; to see the light
Of other days, of earlier centuries . . .
But these improbabilities, though true,
Don't rouse a ripple of awe on the sacred mountain
Where once the Bird that no-one ever saw
Made man kneel down, and cringe, and beg for grace.

THE EIGHTH DAY

I

And on the seventh day,
Having created man in his own image,
He sat back, and from that moment
Never created another thing.—
A pity; on the eighth day, perhaps,
He might have made something better.

II

Dried up? Exhausted? Dead? — or perhaps
He wanted it that way,
And left things incomplete on purpose
When he retired behind the Sun —
When he left his works to manage for themselves.

III

The identical moment never comes again.
Here in the waste-land we do not look for rivers;
And the songs that Schubert never reached —
The unborn music of his Eighth Day —
Can never reach us; they drift
On the River of Ocean, reaching out,
Searching around in vain for alternative routes
From the boundaries of existence,
Exasperated by the scratching noise
Which is all we desert-rats can scrape
From the empty river bed.
"Take us", they cry; "We are brighter than any flood
That ever filled your hearts."
But even when they sing
With all their might, not a sigh
Slips through to our distracted ears,
And the eighth day remains a desert.

PREACHING TO BIRDS

I talk too much;
You might call me a bad security risk.
True, things slip out by chance, not by design.
This morning, for example, I said things
Which hurt Brother Fortune —
A mere slip of the tongue, but the effects
Were much as they would have been with malice.
And it goes on happening:
But, somehow, instead of shutting up
I talk more, and sing, and now
Find myself unloading
All sorts of information; things I had forgotten
And things I did not know I knew.
I keep nothing to myself. —
And it doesn't stop at that; inspired
By the levity that comes of much unloading
I have started throwing out goods and chattels,
And stop thinking about tomorrow's bread and water,
And keep nothing for myself.
The result? I'm turning into a sort of sparrow,
A beggar-bird, able to fly, and — oddly —
Acquiring a knack of catching what other birds say.
Do they trust me? — That would be strange,
Considering what indiscretions
Tumble from my mouth;
Or do they take it that anyone who talks
So freely can't be hiding much, —
And so, talk to me quite freely?
Or do they?
I'm noticing how they answer the big questions
I put to all of them: "Will you believe my words?
Will you do the wishes of the one who made you?"
The eagle says "Fly up here,

You will get a clearer view;"
The parrot says "Will you believe my words?"
The owl says "I see best by night;"
The magpie: "Laugh, man, and you will come to wisdom."
The higher up they fly, the more irrelevant
Their soothing and intelligible replies.
Only the ostrich, who can't fly, keeps to the point;
Which makes me think — whatever benefits
Of weightlessness and readiness for space-flight
I may have gained by all this unloading, perhaps
I talk too much.

EXAMPLES

Strange that Man, the paragon
Of Nature, needs examples
From Nature; that the head
Should ape the lower orders!
But there it is: even
The Book says "Consider
The lilies of the field",
"Go to the ant, thou sluggard".

The ant, a model hero,
Still shames us. — In the bush
My lighted cigarette
Fell on a black river:
Ants; they dug their teeth
Into the *burning* end,
Returning thrust for thrust,
And died without a sound.

And then the spider — mending
Its net for the tenth time:
Gambler, there's your model!
And, sultry lover, yours —
The bridegroom whose act
Of love ends up with him
Inside the bride's body —
Chewed, swallowed and digested;

Model for the devout,
Its attitude of prayer
So fixed, you'd have to break
A limb to interrupt it:
The mantis — whose eyes,
Meanwhile, look round for victims
To tear; a sort of man,
But unperplexed by doubt.

Now look again; those mentors
Can't help themselves, must do
What's written in their cells:
They are the paragons
We emulate, and so
Our deeds need neither heart
Nor head, — only the clockwork
Of a compulsive itch.

IMMORTALS

Not daffodils that hang their heads
   Nor brazen tulips lead the dance:
The modest and the proud give place
   To faceless, microscopic plants —

Invisibles which, all the year,
   Digest, divide and multiply:
While fed they're deathless, leave no corpse,
   But send no flower towards the sky.

Blind soldiers, grey economists,
   You sacrifice both sex and brains,
Put all you have into the fight
   And live immortal for your pains.

We too — our cells, at least — enjoyed
   Such times, had immortality
At first, but step by step evolved
   And learned, at last, to flower and die.

REDUNDANCY

Nature gets away with it:
Repeats each year the same
Familiar alphabet

And utters, without shame,
The clichés she has aired
Since daffodils first came

Before the swallow dared;
Her phrases catch the breath;
We don't ask to be spared

When, having passed through death,
We face the platitude
Of tenth — or fiftieth —

Return to life; have stood
Repeated ecstasies
In the enchanted wood.

Why, then, this quaint disease,
This fever to be new,
This fear we shall not please

With thoughts, however true,
That Man has hatched before?
Are we not Nature too? —

Or is it something more
Than Nature in our kind
Smells out the shapes that bore

As those which will remind
The dying they must die, —
Which, like the solar wind

Unnoticed in the sky,
Corrode the cells, and state
With vast redundancy

The dull routine of fate?

APRIL THE FIRST

Fool's Day, and here — the opening chorus;
Mouths wide open; the only silent parts
Are for the dead and they, at bright moments,
Come half-way back; every fence and stile
Seems able to air new leaves. For a while the old
Wizard repeats his annual round of tricks —
Pulls legs, lambs, chicks out of a hat —
And laughs until the tears run down his cheeks.
"How does he do it? how does he pull it off?"
We murmur; "every year the same patter,
The identical apparitions — but not stale;
Like a refrain, rather than a time-worn tale,
Its touch grows headier with each repetition."
And the magic? — that is real, not fake: search him,
You'll find no chicks or rabbits up his sleeve, —
In fact, you'll find no sleeve; no wizard, even;
Only the magic that from an empty hat
Tips tons of blossom, and the dawn chorus,
And open mouths that threaten to eat up
The struggling harvest and come back for more.
No wonder some will not believe their eyes;
Or make believe they're not impressed, and say
"Let's stuff that rubbish back into the hat."

A GHAZEL

(For Pauline)

From you, my one-year-old, I take some punishment,
A nail or a sock in the eye — with no unkind intent.

But you're so much myself, these casual savageries
Are as though I'd scratched or cut myself by accident.

So much myself? — the soil fosters the rose, and yet
I'd be hard put to find two things as different.

No, not identity, but love — the lines of force
Between contrasted poles — is what I surely meant.

Even now your play won't always fit our rules; you take
What suits you and, for the rest, follow your own bent.

When you learn to speak, strange thoughts will come into your head
Which I fancy you will keep to yourself, being diffident.

In the same way, much later, perhaps, you'll slip from the house;
And who are we to insist on knowing where you went?

You'll have it in you then to inflict worse pain than these
Casual jabs in the eye — though still as innocent.

Start learning to-day, you doting father: such a prize
Was put in trust with you, not given, or even lent.

NECESSITY

(For Miriam)

As if a rooted tree
　　Were suddenly to move,
Or a rock broke free,
　　My daughter, who just now
Was helpless infancy,
　　Suddenly with both hands
Clutched at a stranger's knee
　　And stood for the first time —
Taking this act to be
　　No blinding miracle,
But mere necessity.

NOTHING

(for Ruth)

Her sixth midsummer eve keeps Ruth awake.
The silent house is full of yellow light —
Put out, from time to time, by prowling clouds;
The dripping tap, an unsuspected heart
Somewhere inside the house, seems to grow louder;
Street noises have an unfamiliar ring.
She cannot shut her ears, but even her eyelids
Let through the silent play of light and shade.

At last she leaves her bed and creeps downstairs,
Trembling a little; whispers "I'm afraid."
"Afraid of what?" "Of nothing." When we laugh,
Saying "That means you're not afraid," she cries,
And says, more loudly, "I'm afraid of Nothing;"
Says it again, till suddenly we see it —
Nothing outside the windows; Nothing after
The longest day; Nothing inside the house;
Nothing where everything seemed set for ever.

PHOENIX

Every time I cast my skin
A feebler ghost is left within;

Powers desert me; every year
Some new impediments appear.

Once I shuddered, shut my eyes,
Preferring not to be made wise;

But now I watch my children play
And feel as far from death as they;

For though they threaten to break free
And pity my simplicity,

Insidiously, through leaf and stem,
I have been changing into them.

BREAKING UP

The family is breaking up.
At the seaside, old enough
To care for themselves,
Our children stay at home
When we go out for walks;
And now you, who kept in step
So many years,
Drop behind when I step out.
It's the wrong way round —
The oldest should lag behind;
But as I climb the bare downs
Alone, my mind's ear
Seems to catch your words,
"He has gone first."
A remote, obsessive foghorn
Rubs in the message,
And the white mist around me
Rubs out the wrinkles, flattens
The features of those who pass;
Even my own face
That stares back from a dewpond
Is like one who has gone
Beyond the gates of silence
And has no place on earth.

MIDNIGHT

Casually the lights go out, the doors are locked for the night.
A stray breeze comes and goes, harping on my years
With acid music; now, reminded of the child I was
When that decaying house shone bright with paint and laughter,
I see him wake in peace at midnight, pull aside the curtain —
And there was the familiar street empty and unconcerned,
But with some added meaning I had never caught by day.

Aimlessly I move between the rows of stone faces
With silent eyes and shut lips; and again I catch a phrase
Of that forgotten oracle. On the deserted pavement
The lamps shed such needless light as might be falling now
On Babylon unearthed after the centuries of darkness,
Bare and unearthly as a myth suddenly found to be true,
Or as the quarter-light during the sun's eclipse, from which
The brazen tiger and the mocking jackal slink, afraid.

And I, at this moment, with nothing more than the small change
Of heaven to spend, feel the same peace and agitation
As a child felt with half the truth, its question half-answered
In the green light about as far back as Thebes or Babel,
Those lamplit, familiar cities, tired stone faces
To which my heart rushes home, knowing where to find
The rest of that essential phrase, one answer to all questions.

NOVEMBER

Now, in the second childhood of the year,
The sky floods through these tangled branches
Simplifying, illuminating the tracts
Where once, in longer days, we lost our way;
And, as if more facts would help, the season fires
Rockets of poplar, golden rain of birch —
Fritters away the savings of a lifetime
On fireworks. The few leaves left
Flutter as light and irresponsible
As April foliage, and the urchin tramples
The gold that was, so lately, life itself;
A gale blows up the fallen debris; thunder
Surprises the torpid — shock therapy, a cure
For gloom. These gains are good; the losses — mystery;
Impatience; pride; unrest that had no place
Before the heat of the year.
And here in crackling oakwoods
Of autumn, the rambler with his muddy boots
Turns over an old leaf, gathering
The year's confusion and, for a few moments,
Enjoys a second childhood.

WAITING

Waiting, always waiting for something; once
For birthdays — to grow (or so it seemed)
A whole year older overnight; waiting

For girls, for those who were on time, or others
Who kept you waiting; waiting
For those who never came or came too late;

In queues for trains, or cigarettes, or food;
In waiting rooms for hope, for a bill of health;
Waiting for the signal, for the convulsive siren,

For the all-clear; for the order to push on
Or to pull out — or even to stay put . . .
Waiting for permission to go on waiting; waiting

For buds or doors to open; in the morning
With a dry tongue and eyelids glued together
Waiting for the tired ghosts to dissipate;

Or for the return to a past better than this,
To the springs of hope; for the analgesic memory
Or forgetfulness, whichever you happen to choose;

Waiting for a chance that never comes again
But passes while you are dozing; waiting for sleep
All night; for the eclipse, or for the comet;

Waiting for gifts you have no right to expect,
For gifts or powers once offered, then withdrawn;
Waiting for the will to put up with the second best;

And now waiting for nothing, merely waiting —
And so, in a sense, alive, though a hair's breadth
From where you will not wait for anything.

FULL CIRCLE

Back at the beginning:
Peering without comprehension
At acts and objects;
Hearing with no response
Endearments, exhortations
In single syllables —
The ultimate paraphrases;
Crying on nurse's shoulder,
Or laughing suddenly
Because the sun breaks through;
Unable to contain
Emotion, or to hold
Words or water;
Fretfully refusing
To part with trifles, ornaments,
He strives, none the less,
For independence; leans
Only on the appointed shoulder,
And blessedly mistakes
His child for his mother,
Coming at last full circle
Back to the beginning.

THE SENTENCE

In a faceless queue, two faces,
One sorrowful, one gay:
An aging mother, an infant.
The mother's eyes are drawn
With impotent compassion;
She is younger than she seems
And says nothing. The infant
Is speechless too, but old —
Fifteen, perhaps; a mongol
Who laughs and tries to grab
A shilling in the sky —
The full risen moon.
The mother senses only
A full grown embryo
Beside her, laughing
At the small change of heaven:
Blest like the lion's prey
With numb incomprehension,
He jumps clumsily
On the pavement. — Such joy
In the imperfect one
Turns back the other's anguish
And softens, through the years,
A sentence of hard love.

ENVOI

'Passed over' . . . I thought it meant
  They had forgotten you
And given some pushful type
  Rewards that seemed your due.

But now the word goes round:
  'Dead'. Too late, then,
To repair past oversights;
  They speak the word with pain.

No need: 'through life he hungered
  For the shade; where he has gone
They reward humility
  With a helping of the sun.'

You made your exodus
  From the flesh-pots; to what goal?
What passover could suit
  The deathwish of your soul?

CORRIDA

Explain the mystery:
   As Death approaches near
His pride and majesty
   Crumble and disappear.

The black, outrageous bull
   Bursting upon the crowd
Is cruel and powerful,
   Contemptuous and proud,

Black lightning in his eye
   And thunder in his breath;
Is this the one to die? ——
   He is himself like Death.

Tickled and prodded by
   The darts which won't shake off,
The monster's energy
   Has weakened by a half;

The breathless atmosphere
   Grows lighter, as the bull
Pauses for breath, and fear
   Flits through his empty skull.

Hoodwinked by coloured capes
   A hundred times, the pride
Of Darkness shrinks and gapes;
   Blood trickles down the hide.

Whistling and clapping time,
   Impatient for the kill
Spectators of the crime
   Assert their will.

Shrunken and limp, the beast
    Lunges from side to side.
Cheap music is released. ——
    Death, where is your pride?

Dispassionate and tame,
    He sees the sparkling gilt,
The cape, the sword, the flame
    Which plunges to the hilt.

At last, a sack of meat
    Dragged from the slaughterhouse
And through the empty street,
    He is oblivious.

Explain the mystery:
    As Death approaches near
His pride and majesty
    Crumble and disappear.

DEMONS

Sinners in the old regime
   Had worse to fear than homilies:
   Demons lashed them with disease
And Hell was not an idle dream.

Now those demons have been tamed —
   Not exorcised by priest or pope,
   But sighted through the microscope,
Preserved, and classified, and named.

Things in which men once believed
   Are now crude facts for us to know:
   Belief, in other words, must go
When sober knowledge is received. —

Then, suddenly, some virus broke
   The rules; escaped its cage; turned wild
   Entered the lifestream of a child.
We heard a cry and, shuddering, woke

To see the fever shake those hands,
   The fire break loose — a sudden flash —
   And then the features turn to ash,
The fire to ice. Who understands?

The medicine fails. We know its name,
   But have not whipped that virus out;
   We fly, but can't escape; and doubt
Our senses, but have caught the flame.

Now for a second spell begins
   The age of darkness, and once more
   Demons crouch behind the door,
And pinch our flesh and smell for sins.

FLYING WESTWARD

The clock steals forward, minutes in the hour,
While going west we near the speed of sound
Six miles above the planet;
Fly a bit faster and the clock will stop —
Or seem to stop, while time itself marks time.
Suspended in perpetual sunlight, wrapped
In permanent blue, we peer down and see
A sky beneath us flecked with puffs of cloud,
The smooth Atlantic of an atlas. Tags —
"Motionless movement", "perpetual moment", —
Make sense for once; the audacities of dream
Are coldly real; and yet the mind accepts
This mad excursion as it comes — coldly;
Unmoved in fact by what in fancy rouses
A hurricane.
                    Memories come and go,
And suddenly, a boy, I'm pushed and fall
Into a shallow pond; can't swim, but find
My feet dragging the bottom, and all's well.
Learning to swim, to live, means having first
A foot of solid earth to fall back on:
You get the knack, and soon you're more at ease
Out of your depth; grow lighter and eventually
Discover you can do without the earth,
Without the body, without being . . .
                                        And flight?
You cut the cord, you're launched, and suddenly
The earth below is hell, untouchable,
And here above — until the weather changes
Or till you lose your head — responsive,
In your control, is heaven.
                                As you wake
The weather changes; woolgathering clouds

35

Cover the underworld; winds buffet;
The clock creeps forward, hours in every minute;
All discord is let loose; fear and the gods
Are back, enthroned, — not there above our heads,
But here, all round, beneath us, like those lightnings,
Those following rainbows, like the sky itself.
The gods dictate reliance; drugged, buoyed
By permanent sun, we take delight now
In being passive, resting in the hands
Of the inscrutable. And there below,
Through gashes in the cloud, appears our planet —
A glimpse of the dark world where I was born,
Now savage, canine, rocky; now at ease
With lawns or forests; now built up, lit up.
Out of our depth, we drift and slowly drop
Through space down to the somnolent Pacific,
And stare due west toward the map's Far East.

ABSENCE

(for A)

Absent from you so long, I begin to feel
As though, somewhere, I had passed a one-way door
And joined the dead who, unwillingly, keep their distance.

'Distant', 'absent' . . . those muted bells
Keep beating on my nerves. Last night I dreamed
Of the dead; they sat apart, estranged, indifferent:

Could it be that I might haunt your dreams like that?
The thought breaks through me like a sunless wave;
I wake myself with a shout on the point of drowning.

Here with blandishments of smiling air
And luminous towers, I seem to be disembodied,
At times feel I have reached the timeless world;

On scheduled flights pick out white peaks beneath me;
In the blue upcast light the baby-faced
Attendants seem like blest, translated spirits.

By stages, though, the smile becomes a leer,
The harmony swells to a crashing discord,
The celestial spectrum shows itself a spectre.

Because the act, though meaningless, brings comfort,
I call your name as though the sound might reach you,
And stretch my hands eastward in your direction;

Surely this river, Time, on which I drift,
Though seeming to be motionless, is moving,
Slowly at times, then faster, sometimes racing

Or tumbling over crags, through stony channels,
Drifting me closer to the heady moment
When from this after-life I return to you.

ASTROLOGY

"The desire of the moth for the star . . .
Shelley

So it's true, all that nonsense
About the stars controlling destiny:
True, anyway, for migrant birds!
The black-cap in a planetarium
(Try the experiment — you'll find it works)
Flies north, not south, in Autumn
If you rotate his 'sky' through half a circle;
Will sleep, on actual flights, by day; will break
His journey on some barren crag or twig
When clouds obscure the constellations; —
True, too, for migrant moths
Which fly towards a star —
And singe their wings at lamps that look like stars.

But we, who make a boast of understanding,
Have lost — or never had — the knack
That moths and geese and pigeons take for granted;
Those wise men from the East, who found their way
By starlight to the birth at Bethlehem,
Were granted powers, perhaps, ahead of schedule
For man, though natural to fly or fowl;
Why cast such patronising looks
On animals because they are dumb
And ignorant of what they are?
We are as ignorant of how one finds
A route by starlight or in utter darkness;
And though we learn our maps and get to know
Where Sirius shines and where to find Orion,
The star-led geese which fly to their salvation
Are hatched with all that wisdom in their heads.

IN CAMERA

I

The square is full of people, but this eye —
A camera slung around my neck,
The proverbial witness which can tell no lie —
Proves that, in fact, there are no people here:
Shutting out almost all the light and keeping
The film unmoved, I take, at intervals,
A score of photographs of the same view
To make one single picture: here it is —
The picture of an empty square! The doors
And windows of Renaissance palaces,
The statues, lamp posts, fountains, flowers are true
To life, but not one human form is there,
Except for something like a ghost leaning
Against this column . . . .
                              and another thing —
Not noticed till one looks a second time:
There are no hands on the great city clock.

II

Something like a ghost,
Or else (more commonly)
Nothing; — that's the most

An eye in harmony
Only with the permanent
Can see of man: to see

This phantom we are lent
Another sort of eye
Tuned to the transient . . .

And yet, what passes by
May (though it disappear)
Not be the first to die:

'There shall not be left here
One stone upon another . . . . '
The trumpet scatters fear,

While from the four winds gather
The swift, the slow; the lean,
The sluggish; those who bother,

Or who ignore: unseen, —
Mere phantoms to the sense
In which stone columns mean

Something like permanence, —
But gifted to survive,
To turn experience

To their own ends; to dive
And swim where most will drown;
To multiply, and thrive

When walls are thrown down.

MIRRORS

They can't lie; there is no virtue in it
When mirrors tell you nothing but the truth.
Twenty times a day
I catch a glimpse of my reflected frown
Which tells me nothing I don't know already —
Too much at that: the arteries
Which wind like rivers at my temples;
The lines of life extending
Like spiders' webs over my wrists and knuckles;
The cross I carry on my brow . . . .
Catching a glimpse of it
I quickly change the expression
To a sheepish smile, then turn my back abruptly
On the ungracious mirror.

No critic is more candid,
No witness more infallible — for the candid
And those possessed with sanity,
The fluke we take so casually for granted.
So it was with you, my lost companion,
Till one day, when you least expected it,
That model of all candour
Sprang a surprise upon you —
Retorted with a face you did not know;
And when you moved, responded
With quite a different movement —
A frown in answer to a smile; a nod
Because you shook your head;
And then, in case you'd think
The oracle now spoke by opposites —
Giving you scope to do something about it —
Remained unmoved when you threw up your arms.
You were held, of course, to blame

For the unpredictable antics,
The reflections in a mutinous mirror;
It would have turned the wits of wiser men
To be judged for crazy things they'd never done.

What happened then?
What mute explosion? fatal exploration
Inside the skull, to the volcanic centre?
Left groping at the surface,
We tried to follow, but gave up;
Shouted your name, but got no answer;
Fed you by force in case you starved to death —
Till suddenly you hit upon the cure:
Changed roles, and started waiting for the mirror
To make the first move.

IN THE HEADLAMPS

Submerged Atlantis and the coral reef;
   Ruins of Memphis, Corinth; capitals
   Burned out, deserted, nothing left but shells;
Snatches of childhood fantasy or belief
Blaze in the headlamps which pick out each leaf
   For a moment. A shadow dreaming at its post
   Springs to attention — lightning more than ghost —
And throws the background into black relief.
As much dead as alive, stock still
   In that enchanted wood, the cattle wait
For darkness to feed on and have its fill;
      And now I see, almost without surprise,
      Two tiny headlamps facing mine — the eyes
Of a lone tomcat by some garden gate.

SOMETHING MORE

Always looking around for something more
   Than meets the eye, for an apparition,
God or angel, suddenly I find it —
   In everything that meets the eye
But hides so much more than it ever shows.

Now, in the eye's light,
Everything for a moment is translated
From the molecular language
To simple words, to shapes I understand,
At once familiar and unfamiliar;
And men are gods, and animals are angels.

BIRMINGHAM ROTUNDA

Where carious chimneys reeked — an empty sky:
In the place of sky — this impossible tower!
The thing had escaped my thoughts, when suddenly
Through mist it sprang to attention; was it there
An hour ago when I looked in that direction? —
It hasn't encroached on the sky inside my skull,
But wears the unwholesome gleam of apparition.
So now a job like one they left unfinished
At Babel is complete in the flicker of an eye.
A portent? perhaps this — that having bridged
The gap and reached their heaven of material glory
Its makers are still cut off from the other world —
Kept at a distance by the bridge itself:
One gesture holds heaven up and holds it off.

THROUGH CLOUDS

As if they could see through the clouds and catch
    The sun's eye, these fields carpeted
    With buttercups seem to reflect the sunlight
That's hidden from our eyes. May is a match
For its opponents, making clairvoyants
    Of its tried favourites, who pass the message
    To us and fill our eyes with golden light,
So that we too feel favoured. But if chance
Finds us in a flowerless patch, the green
    That glows so much the deeper for these downpours
    Casts an illusion that we are looking out
Through sunglasses on a much brighter scene.

DAYLIGHT ASTRONOMY

(for John Press)

Daylight astronomy: the lark, a fixed star
Above your head, stays much of the morning
At one spot; the starlings in their courses
Punctually cross the zenith; swifts dive
Like meteors; and the owl asleep in a branch
Looks out of place, like a moon in the morning sky.
Prompting their movements elemental forces,
Mass and acceleration, gravity,
Love, hunger, fear quietly interact.

Meanwhile a speck of light is barely crawling
With ominous silence, trailing a white wake
Across the blue. At once we recognise
The comet loaded with a terrible secret,
And try to look away or shut our eyes,
But seem to grasp its orbit through shut eyelids;
No symbol or equation can express
That orbit, or unravel what it means,
The paradoxical writing on the sky.

But those huge nebulae, the clouds which hide
Our sun and send astronomers to bed,
Give comfort. For while covering the shapes
That scare or baffle us, they stifle fear
And quench perplexity; until it seems
That, like the residents of Venus, screened
By permanent clouds from anything beyond,
We can doze on, unruffled by the risks
Of fusion, fission, radiation, fire.

THE YAWN

Cautiously, as the alarm bell fizzles out, I open eyes,
    First one, then another; next my mouth opens —
In a wide yawn; wordless, but a mode of communication,
    Meaning "Sleep, come back; you are better than what happens".

At the peak of day, a yawn, meaning "Get on with it!" —
    On the racetrack; in the queue; held up at a level crossing
Or a door marked "Engaged" . . . While the best minutes
    Tick past, lost for good — a yawn to mark their passing.

Afternoon: I nod over documents and yearn
    For a dip in the cool stream; my yawn means "Die,
Torments of choice!" Now the murmuring heat outstrips me;
    For a moment I dream I'm swimming in the upturned sky.

At night, though, drained but fulfilled I yawn luxuriously,
    Sucking the darkness, satisfied with love and taking pain
Or death as fair payment for creation; now send me
    Oblivion before I begin to find fault again.

TRIUMPHAL ARCH

Hope, rainbow, the triumphal arch
That none alive goes under,
Appears, rare but real,
To the footsore, the uncertain,
With news of a new planet;
A phantom, but intenser
Than house, rock, hill
Of the land it overhangs;
Annunciation of all
That seemed too far, too good.

But we, who stand transfigured by the glow,
Transfixed by the apparition,
Feel no necessity
To pass through the elusive arch:
Seeing the black clouds
Beyond it and the sun
On our side, we know
We have already marched
Under those very colours
And reached the better side.

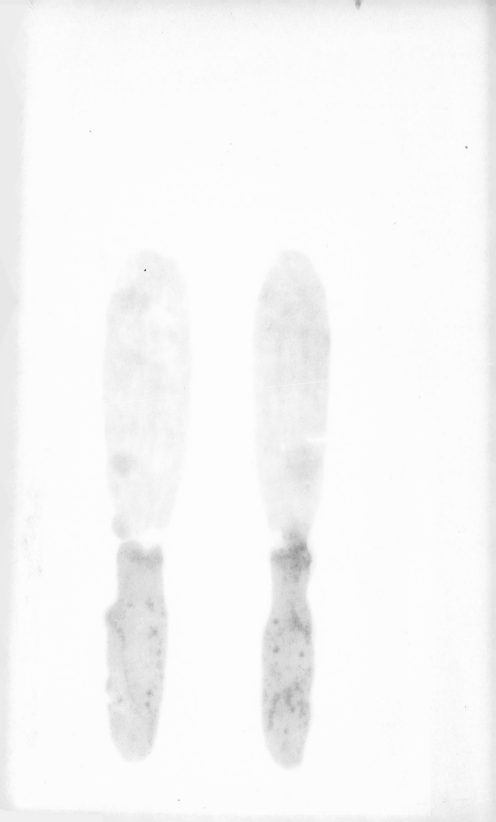

DATE DUE

GAYLORD   PRINTED IN U.S.A.